Ianthe Poems

Peter Philpott

Ianthe Poems

Shearsman Books

First published in the United Kingdom in 2015 by
Shearsman Books
50 Westons Hill Drive
Emersons Green
BRISTOL
BS16 7DF

Shearsman Books Ltd Registered Office
30–31 St. James Place, Mangotsfield, Bristol BS16 9JB
(this address not for correspondence)

www.shearsman.com

ISBN 978-1-84861-417-8

ACKNOWLEDGEMENTS
Much of the *Ianthe Poems* have appeared
in Andrew Jordan's *10th Muse*,
online in *Veer-About* (edited by Adrian Clarke and William Rowe),
on Edmund Hardy's *Intercapillary Space* website,
and online in Stephen Emmerson's *blart.*

CONTENTS

for Ianthe Judith Smith-Spark
(b. September 16, 2009)

The desire to tell within the conditions of a discontinuous consciousness seems to constitute the original situation of the poem. The discontinuity of consciousness is interwoven through the continuity of reality – a reality whose independence of our experience and descriptions must be recognized. In response, the poetic impulse, attempting (never successfully) to achieve the condition that the phrase "language and 'paradise'" names, seeks to extend the scope and temporal continuity of consciousness.

—Lyn Hejinian, *The Language of Inquiry*
(University of California Press, 2000), p 77

Speculations

Bertan jaio naizen arren,
Ez dut ezagutzen nire herria.
Nire hizkuitza bera duen arren,
Ez dut ulertzen nire herria.

Felipe Juaristi, "Geografia"

1

What you read is here
open at its jaws
like a really killer simile
can you believe? the facts
are the things made
and make us oh like words
uncoiling and beginning to glisten
I love this world for appearances
shining shining shining
and sometimes sounding
a far off deep hum
or the lilt of actual voices
can you hear it?
oh, do not fear this caress

what you read here is
what wisdom in these words
uncountable but singable not
what is said but how
each word points at this world!
here is what you read in fact
oh what a big and complicated text
who made it?
we did, then, every bit
I love its punctuation marks
we can only do it once
oh beautiful world
utterance must quietly end
brief as the shining sun

2

Be careful of the poets
they can't always know
just the clumsy algorithms for perception
what did you expect then?
I can't tell you what is at the centre
something is very circumscribed
here is metaphysics and history
words like days and bodies
unrepeatable and separate

be careful of the poetry
it lies
in lines and verses
a sort of unprogressive dialectic
nothing at its centre
but an influx suddenly of meaning
sometimes of its lack
a great shadow
turns off the light

3

Who turned this line around
setting its repetitive trudge here
to open at the ragged headlands
like a hand of nine fingers
all the more for solace
the question drops ungrudging into evening
a dear clear light
transparent and remorseless as your gaze
unconvinced of causation

back like a little patient ox
I am harnessed to good labour
up here above the town
little and bright like a toy
this sight will give solace
as the night grows into the unquestioning
of course you must play
this game is serious
it must convince you of causation

4

But be still and sleep now
growth comes in the night
something here is very quick
and the heavens mean nothing to us
rumours of colossal machines
that vast space you will grow into
at its edge where we were born
your sleeping eyes track the body inside
oh let the lights swing crazily around

and now still sleep but be
resting unpredicated
wordless

like a missed beat an
influx of that joke
bursting at our hearts
uncertain and miscounting
some fine shadow games

5

The pressure to think and sing
who said that?
not really a manichee but
these unsubtle dialectics will suffice
bursting out in farts and hiccups
diverse encounters with the uncontrollable
we are placed within all this
like in night and day
the problems are all the night

all night that pressure then?
an hysteria in the dark
you live within these intensities
the secular shifts ignored
each beat counts
the world crystallises around
like ice on our windows
sign that cold queen has visited
our problem within our night

6

This is where the old lines
playing in the darkness with
a deep full-bodied song
thrums and redoubling it will ascend
the green lanes
what ought to be shining here?
all our quick voices
running like wild animals
some exercise in hydrostatics

following the pistons
off into the darkness
where song ranges through its gamut
ascending like the sun
shining above the green lanes
out into some utopian fantasy
buy into this or perish!
corralled with psychographic isoclines
plunge into the masses now

7

Music plays quietly here
machines hum and gurgle gently
it is an adverbial attention
let's illumine the substantives!
hiding in each shadow
all pocketed up so cosy
like babes in hoods with ears
each little connotation we love
brightly as violins

can anyone remember what came before?
now only a single constant present
that is a nice thing to give to us
so gravely done
like a hand reaching out from the shadow
to tuck us up one last time
hoods up! connotations
tied tight!
what is this brightness now?

8

It wavers as the floor shakes
I dreamt of the supermarket
this was the story of the Red Thief
– glistening
deep colours remain as solace
what there is bright and empty
the suspended floor thrums and wavers
you step out and declare
this will end now

it doesn't
go on unsaying it
like how does it doesn't?
no wonder this place shakes
trying to free itself from the light pouring
no solace then
a slow crawl or scrunch
real things always alliterate
the Red Thief thought

9

The shining is at the window
yellow in one room and blue in another
can you see colours yet?
or what can you see that's not identifiable
unbounded and nameless
like a big voice speaking over
us yes I'm including you in
this is totality it
too shimmers

the games are at the window
yellow in one game and blue in another
can you see games yet?
or what can you see that's not games
unbounded and games
like big games speaking over us
yes I'm including games in this
is games
shimmering far in excess

10

In all things trust rain
you will have no choice
swaddled and cosseted
it is good fortune to be a cat
this is about the opening of the novel
where the heroine enters naked and screaming
no, this isn't a joke
it all happened one night
surrounded greyly with rain

no not game
open the door! open the door!
swaddled against these intensities it
is your good fortune to be ignored
an unobserved grin flickers across
something really has entered, crystallised out
like frost on windows on the first night maybe
you will be that queen
you are now limpid, gurgling as water

11

Oh let that sunshine in
beautiful old lemons
she, the sun, loves us so much
hands pinch and stroke
hopping over us on their little feet
I am not green
I am pink and shining
I smell of sleep
quiet unconfinement

no, no, not that sunshine
bouncing between us and the sky
she, the sun, doesn't see us
we are out of her hands entirely
something new has entered
shining in our sleep like a knife I
can't remember the green lanes
the smells of animal panic
now quieted, unconfined

12

Today I am eating a mince pie
sometimes a speech act is just so predictable
some obvious common factor
at your school it will be different
wearing your dark hoods in the shadows
svelte and slightly threatening
for you Christmas will be
oh, just another old pagan festival
how glorious and unpredictable it shall be

not a poltergeist but a plumber
make each speech act distinct and memorable
like a many-cornered prime number
yes, you'll learn about these one day
casting their blue light from the shadows
surprising but unthreatening like some kid in a hoodie
suddenly here at Christmas
no one else but an old geezer
how glorious and unpredictable it is

13

I am sitting under a small tree
sometimes poems are true
these are the constantly surprising ones
they tell us about this night
and what is unobserved
your daily growth
an intricate game you play out
look – you're learning!
does this tree amuse you?

will you be amused by the true?
reach out with an indomitable taxis
hold! hold! – aahhh
there is a lot of repetition in it
boring prosy bits I know
the connections grow inside quietly
a whole new cosmos
you release through your eyes and mouth
almost unobserved into this night

14

This night is unobserved through cold
white and black
what entered: a mocking cloth or shroud
some things are made to just finish us off
this is the total estrangement of what we had hoped for
pretty, shining
set within such varied lines
lanes, trains – don't trust
crunching

what entered was true
moving slowly because of the
cold ah! now she does and shines
repeating back our loss
it enters like a cat
it's hunger blocks us off
but a whole new green world
touch it!
still unconfined, tremulous and glad

15

How glorious the sky!
the simplicity of covering everything
she was perfectly lucid of course
it wasn't a day when anything was meant though
let's just see where this takes us
look! to the horizon
lost in a shadow like a big hood
no, no bunny ears on this one
but footsteps crunching

it was truth coming in
moving slowly because of the
cold now she hides in the shadow
repeating back our loss
hey! no – the cat in the hood
its hunger blocks us off
but a whole new glorious world
touch it!
its footsteps still crunching

16

It's always more like sleet and slush
tuck yourself up now little one
a nice warm bunny suit gives good solace
our English ways are so full of mire and rubbish
your little vehicle shakes from side to side don't
sleep now! despite the cold
later, later when the dark time comes
rage a little like you always do
then sleep out this whole cold night

the sky is polished with sulphur and lead
a repeated alchemical processing
the laying down of the little one
it gives more solace than sleep
gently agitates the soul
winnows out the dreck and rubbish
so we are borne as dumb and hairy beasts
tucked up into nature
gentle crisp coverlets of dirty snow

17

Bless the pramstrings of our hearts! the
empress of all the mice has supped all
the noisy games of excess passed this
is a simple quiet day
a faint grey drizzle like contentment
do you want to remember?
oh you want to fly off and eat
frolic long on this cold shore
before night opens again

before this period obtrudes on heaven
that excess overlaps a tall music here: sol-fa!
above their noisy games, oh excess passionate
the I astonishes some quickening desires
any foolish games die, lacking content
didn't youth welcome this resilience?
our Yulish wanderings their footsteps all exceeded
fun longs outside the crisp shadows
beating noisy old anguish

18

Oh dear the blackbird is attacking!
the dear little blackbird swoops and glides
he descends as suddenly as night
you think you are unobserved
sheer quarrelsomeness spreading amongst the birds
why don't we plan our next growth?
we could fly from true to tree
our frolics startling and silly but
it'll all stop when, you know

some little creatures rest at this season
stir occasionally, with small cries
above their noisy games, unobserved growth
the astonishment of quirky desire
only the foolish games die
youth welcomes full resilience
we wander through this Yulish night
fun lingers outside the shadows
please no more anguish now, little blackbird

19

And how are we at latching on?
unconfined and hesitant – eager body noises
though we all of us wait at this time
I forget when the last poem entered
then when the sun was shining above the green
your little joys are good enough for spring
it's all seeking solace in embodiment
jolly frolics to drag us through the day
the point where it really stops comes much later

your little rests are of your nature
your unconfined small cries
unobserved and always resilient you grow
astonishment entered the room with you
though the green dies, you will blossom
you will welcome for us the shining spring
the solace of your embodiment a crackling log
you make the shadows dance
may their crazy lengths give you no anguish now

20

You'll be shown after tomorrow
isn't that expected then?
imagine the kings in glorious hoods
crunching out of their shadows it'll
be quick as an inoculation
and you'll sleep after
the cold furry body of this world dreaming
the desperate frolics of the birds no stop –
just unwearying change

can you live the same day twice
I can't blame you for the birds in their plight
the strength of the body grows under this rime
it'll all come back and astonish
we shall preserve you from harm
crunching over the shadows
casting your hood back, glorious
isn't that expected?
see! here! let's give you this day

21

A true Christmas babe would be born from Easter
we'll wrap you up as something else
the present is what we actually are doing
subject to the weather dying down
it's a funny old time before rebirth
little solace, many shakes, none gentle
eternity's crisp breath sublimes us
quick let's fly inside your embodied dreams
then we shall never weary of change

can you write the same poem twice?
I can't blame you for the birds in their flight
the body grows stronger without rhyme it'll
all come back in our stories
this shall preserve you from harm
send you off with gentle shakes
ah! solace of our barest rhythms
wasn't that expected?
see! hear! let's grow today!

22

The cat covets the jungle gym
you make us ooze emotion, then feed
I think it's time to get back to the present
we are pressed into by its excess
awaiting something noisy and plenary
a series of games – let them all escalate
eternity's crisp breath shall bring anguish
we can't really enter your dreams
but must never weary of change

how can the present just carry on its being?
why don't things fly apart like noisy birds?
yes, the baby will grow stronger through her games
she sheds herself as she imagines
at this excess an anguish, oh despite
ssshh! let's send you off now, little small
repeating sotto voce words like 'solace' and
'dearest' what is expected can be miraculous
see and hear, here this dark season

23

No poem yet on piss and shit
in fact liquids spout, ooze at every opening
you are bathed in your own growth, a little grub
oh foolish in the night because
oh nothing that hasn't happened elsewhere, unobserved
you know, like what isn't in this poem
so just how many changes then today?

wrapped up and bundled smelling pink and clean
the foolish birds can fly inside you, little one
you will grow stronger through the night
the unobserved make and remake these things a constant
          present
ssshh! this growth replenishes also us
what is expected miraculous
see, hear, taste – no anguish now, little blackbird

Bishops Stortford
October 28, 2009 – January 5, 2010

Noting Nothing

Let's write with this pen
its words aren't of course these things
writing in blue on a small page
stripping off the lines
fearfully
slowly ooze
down that page

not this one

calm and all at once
a lying creation
(like it all is)

like a sleeping child
like a child's hand
cast and metallised
an omen of death

oh, the hectic and provisional slidings
repeated & unrepeatable
messy art of human making

It was the mazurka I heard
sliding through the quiet rain of a Sunday morning
everything grey and green
                    dull tweedy days

How joyful to write on this English
spring that muddy slide out of death
How perfect
like a Radio 3 soundtrack
to write so defiantly non-avant-garde

look! the bluebells are little tiny dots
          swirling into a numinous haze

What is outside the text
is mainly rain right now
with some secondary drips
and a lot of splashable deposition still
inescapable as the pull of gravity
the sheer shape of our poor tongue thus
dropping us back here

The Labour Party poster glows sadly in the window
David Tibet's voice swirls around
rhyming death & resurrection

that's not likely now

Persistent bird cries
like little lyric poems
erupt, delight then bore
lie at the back of our being
insistently reminding us of being
overflowing
around us
like grace

for if there is a God
she may be a blackbird

hence her love for beetles

How the silence bounces about the café
– only briefly mind
it's a busy hill
& besides in quiet times
the staff need this music
cool & soggy as the cakes, alas

There's also the floor
– most of this is floor
worn as it is
good planking
heavily used
the varnish now matt
worn off to light wood
pale & dead

it holds the weight
it holds the noise

it doesn't
hold the silence
spilling & breaking
inside & here

I object the television's noise
because I regret the red shoe
oh! It was beautiful
        that
        simply

        beautiful
        like a lovely spangly thing

        the sea
        say

        or a model tracing out brain activity
        as we think of constellations

oh it shone that fierce!

it is what I love

enfolded like consciousness

Oh no the man on the silver motor scooter rode on
by

– has he stolen the laptop
  I am writing this poem on or by

  I am writing it about
  he is faster than me
  (most people are
  you are I
  am sure
  nothing
  couldn't
  be

  he
  comes
  back to me
  swinging through
  the whole town
  singing & zooming
  like a great baby
  swinging through the heavens
  fat & giggly & slobbering
  the whole silver arc so swift
  it was easy to see
  how this laptop could be taken
  and the window
                     breaks

Where is the tooth now?
All I can feel
        is the hole

           warm sunshine
           & light that bounces
           sharp & aggressive

there are only the splinters of a world here
one we know will soon come to its end
it'll all be over by Christmas they say
and then
        nothing

        like a great hole
        like a trick of the light

But the tooth is out there!

        lost, broken
        at least partly
        metaphorical

The anomalous milkbottle balances
like any other projection of a mental state:
frequent fracture! frequent fracture!
You know it will happen.
I do wash them as I hope you do
to hurry up their stainless transmigrations
My grandmother was a goose, you know

> a glassy one
> glaucous

Has this taken you where you didn't expect?
It usually happens on rebirth like this
everything comes together, well, just not the same
– that really would have been silly, yes?
to imagine a crystalline purity remaining
flawless like a new glass bottle while
all around galaxies whirl and stars die

Just silica dust communicating
at the red end of the spectrum

Ah! thinking of fields of barley I listen to Schumann
– all that

       what?

       a gradual desiccation

       that horn part did mean something
       then

       a car draws up
       I am very vulnerable now

               you know
               to any
               passing off

       the horns! the horns!

crescendi wave like corn
what drives them?

such delivery   such decay

old dirty water plunges
Siena lies open in its decay

how fondly we recall that little red funicular
and maybe it will remember us

off into the woods we go
some like animals, some like birds

If we debate
     furiously like a sandstorm
     fields of flarf v. conceptual acidity
     what Thing at the heart or core?
     like the little grain
          at the gobstopper's core
     still & silent while the colours wear off
     a long hot day spent in reaching it
     again & again repetition is a pleasure
     not a brisk one at all
     slightly desperate maybe but
     childhood & poetry are like that
                     aren't they?

Here is the non-poetic coffee shop
where babies gather in their buggies
& a man gives a tutorial on public health
as the staff chat about what they bought on holiday

– this tedium is so clear, luscious
knowing it may not last & we may not
meet here again, our set of metaphors
unravel & explode

– no, there won't be time for a break
or wondering what flavours we haven't tried, for
as all this comes to its end
maybe slowly
maybe surely
& the babies grow up (if they're lucky)
& there is health to pursue and make public
or that we will ever take ease elsewhere

our ease is sweet here
luscious and dropping

The boy ate the wooden ball
He ate it well. He read
"Notes on Conceptualisms" as he did
then ate that too

Where in this
is the wooden ball?
Not
of course
in this poem
but in the Community Hall
packed up I think in a plastic tub
while the book
which I haven't yet read
might be above the Atlantic now

How brave this world of new poetry
is! The whole universe opens like it
lies to the toddler's eager grasp
incapable of separating fantasy and thing
but then again
who would?

Bishops Stortford/London/Tuscany,
March-November, 2010

Dubbadea
Mummy, Daddy, Babby

...poetry belongs in the same realm as vocabulary, myth, and figures of speech. Far from taking its authority from the poet's genius, poetry, despite the poet's existence, is a sort of authorless speech. It has no locator; it is what "is said." ... poetry has no more of an author than vocabulary does. It resembles myth, and the profound reason that makes the Greeks say that a poet by definition create myths is perhaps linked ... to the fact that myth and poetry draw their authority from themselves. The truth comes from the lips of poets as naturally as it issues from those of children. They do nothing but reflect things as they are.

—Paul Veyne, *Did the Greeks Believe in Their Myths?*
An Essay on the Constitutive Imagination
(trans. Paula Wissing), University of Chicago Press,
Chicago & London, 1988, p 64

1

Oh look
  our mother did this

  birds haunt the flowers
  the monkey on the mandolin

  they hop around
  cheerily they call

  blossoming at last
  into such multiplicity

  like clouds
    swags of silk
    that's our sky above

  is it there?

  so beautiful
  & real

  oh as weather

snow and light
the big yellow sun
let's start there

2

or here?

so many little ones
spilling out & frolicking
the vessels are emptied now
so let's run & play

& use again
the word multiplicity
something like love
heaping us with fullnesses &
feeling tottering among the flowers
                                        feeding

There is a single simple joy
it doesn't know what it is
holds on & pleasures

there isn't any knowing

run around the wind here

3

These words are fieldfares

    flying out
    and hopping

    their various patternings

    – how do I know this
    when I'm only one or so?

    oh who
          is nearer
                  to our great matrix
then?

    oh fly off
          waves of music
          in hidden beautiful intelligence

                    grace
               delight-giving

    the gross conceit of flight
    scattered & harmonious

    look! look!

      or listen

4

A happy silence
>> w/ distant shrieks
>> oh ex**cite**ment!

>> this happens

>> the placing
>> coming from
>> the feeling
>> that bursts
>> as a
>> new form

>>> a new form!
>>> of excitement!

But still a happy silence
Write quietly
This is a form of absence
>> a silence
>> or opening
>> that isn't
>> silence but
>> lies underneath
>> that

>> the darkness enclosing
>> that too
>>> born into

*   *   *

& what care
attendant is possible
in this world?

maybe sentences
can't see them
what you hear
        goes on for ever

        where does it come from
        then?
                well?
    drawn up out of some green abyss
slow life & deep
pressure it dances
        all of it

this its music?
more other tones
good humour to expand

sleep through
as well sleep
right through this world
          here

*   *   *

Oh the shrieks of those French children
their noises are disgusting
                    fascinating
                    unhomelike

they're only visitors
here in & out
            like sparrows etc
            (sort of lovable
                        but outside this tight circle
                        just other people
                        as good as dogs

                        bears are best
                        but rarely seen alas!
                        in these streets

                        then cats – great
                        Milliband and Mopsy Cat
                        strange relatives
                        (but aren't we all
                        padding through this world too
                        where it builds itself up
                        unknowingly

*   *   *

oh the singing of those free children
their noses are disgusting
          facing us and
          gnomish like

unthanked
their own visas to here
in art
     asparagus
     soluble
        bitter

        outside this tight circles
        justice is people
        as wooden clogs

        bears are burnt
        unseen
        in these streets

        the catch?
        great mulligatawny mops
        strangled to live
        bitter!
        moving into wobbles to
        where it's busy
        uneasily

* * *

all that snot & spit
blubbering & repetition
like foreign children

aspergerish
         soluble
         and bitter

it begins to sparkle!

bears are best their
shit is wooden then
cats
         ferociously digging

         total ritual
         yet to convince
         enacting what?

let's grow
into this new world

where we shall throng
         w/ fieldfares & babies

*   *   *

Oh in some far field
                  full of birds
                     or boots
                  little roots

                          gently gently

                        These children now
          are free

5 I & I is I

I see daddy
at work I see

        words
        see pictures
        pictures of words
        I

I feed
I admonish
I put in order

I, I, I

minute & repetitive
striking this whole world
into its existence
blossoming in its spring
literally and obviously

I see these words

I slip between them
from one

        to one
        and I
        am the

6

or here?

all the babbas
run around
shout like birds
they fly

all at once
lots of ways
like love
heaped spoonfuls
tottering among flowers
are feeding

oh simple joy
no knowing
hold on in pleasure

no – no knowing now

    run around shout
    in joy little brown
    birds & babies

7

along
comes something

mummy & daddy &

birds, flowers, monkeys, mandolin

call out in clarity, hilarity,
    charity I am the

each one blossom
this only universe

a big cloud, a foam
big warm fuzziness
swagging about us
like the sky or the earth
or like language
slowly entered
carefully like a simile
    first a smile

oh like water all about us
    always that
we're only born here once
   here now the
  Ianthe

Bishops Stortford
October 2010 – April, 2011

Notes

Epigraph to *Speculations* from ed. (& trans.) Mari Jose Olaziregi,
Six Basque Poets (Arc, 2007)
> "I was born here,
> yet I don't know this place.
> We speak the same language,
> yet I don't understand my people."

Some Explications
Many of the poems were written in coffee shops, then often of
necessity when taking Ianthe out, for her daytime naps in the
buggy.

Green Lanes, running from Harringay to Stoke Newington, repre-
sent the cattle-drove route to Smithfield.

on p 17, "The pressure to think and sing" – a phrase from Keston
Sutherland.

on p 20, "the story of the Red Thief" – "a story for which the world
is not yet prepared".

Music invoked or heard includes p 54, Current 93, "This Shining
Shining World" on *Of Ruine or Some Blazing Starre (The Broken
Heart of Man)*, & p 48, Schumann, *Konzertstück for Four Horns in
F, Op. 86*.

On p 52, Vanessa Place & Robert Fitterman, *Notes on Concept-
ualisms* (Ugly Duckling Presse, 2009), a book probably small
enough to be eaten, but liable to make your belly bitter I'd think.

Dubbadea starts with an image from Salomon Trismosin, *Splendor
Solis* (1582; Harley 3469) – online images at <http://www.hermetics.
org/solis/solis.html > ("The Hermetics Resource Site") – plate 20,
"Ludus Puerorum".